1

Rough Country Trading Post
P. O. Box 127
Dinosaur, Colorado 81610.
Wagner, John

Corona, the Golden Boy & His Band
2nd Edition, March 6, 2015

Book design by John A Wagner
Photographs by John A Wagner

Also by John A Wagner

First Flight- Journey of a Man and an Eagle

The Magnificent Wild Mustangs of Sand Wash Basin

Picasso: Wild Stallion of the West

The Bird Herd of Sand Wash Basin

Fighting Stallions of Sand Wash Basin

Frightful Freefall's Photo Album

Foxy Foxes

The Legend of Jericho Jones

Run Son, Run Series

Run Son, Run

Run Son, Run part 2

Run Son, Run part 3

To Boldly Go Where No Horse Has Gone Before part 4

To Boldly Go Where No Horse Has Gone Before part 5

# Corona: The Golden Boy and His Band

## by John A Wagner

When you see Corona for the very first time, you immediately think of him as a palomino but Corona is a Dunalino, because of the dorsal stripes down his back, and the zebra stripes on his legs.

At the time I wrote this book, Corona had 11 in his band.
Their names are: Lona, Maybell, Bobby, Can Wakan-2011 filly, Cheyenne, Em, One Spirit, Indian Rose, Indiana Jones- 2011 colt, Yampatika and Tecate.

Corona takes excellent care of his band. He knows Sand Wash Basin like you know your own backyard.  Corona knows where the best grazing is at and where the waterholes are and he is very protective of his band.

Everyone that goes to Sand Wash Basin looks mostly for these two Band Stallions, Corona and Picasso.

Make sure you put Sand Wash Basin on your Bucket list of places to go to.

Happy Trails My Friends

John Wagner

**Corona the Golden Boy**

**Cheyenne**

**Corona and Band**

**Em**

**At the waterhole.**

**Corona and Indiana Jones**

**The Golden Boy "Corona."**

**Little "Can Wakan" and Lona.**

**"Who's That?"**

**"I'm ready to run, are you?"**

![Corona and Band]

**Corona and Band**

**Cheyenne**

**Prancing**

**Cosmo & Corona sizing each other up!**

**Can Wakan (Sun Dancer in Lakota Sioux).**
**Did you notice all four hoofs off the ground?**

**The Awesome Golden Boy.**

**Close Family Shot.**

**Another Family shot.**

**Cheyenne**

**Corona**

**Indiana Rose**

**Can Wakan**

**Corona**

**Tecate**

**Corona, Em & One Spirit**

**Mr. Golden Boy**

**"The Lake"**

I hope you have enjoyed this photo book on Corona and His Band.

Be sure and put the wild horses of Sand Wash Basin in Northwestern Colorado on your bucket list of things to do.

Happy Trails,

John A Wagner

John A Wagner lives in the little town of Dinosaur, Colorado with his wife Sarah, daughter Megan & their dog Buddy.

One of John's favorite pastimes is photographing the wild horses of Sand Wash Basin.

As John says, "Heaven to the Cowboy was spending time on the open range where he could talk to God in his own way."